Cultism to Charisma

CULTISM
TO
CHARISMA

My Seven Years with Jeane Dixon

Alice Braemer

with DOLORES HAYFORD

and with a Foreword by Ruth D. Nickel

Exposition Press   Hicksville, New York

This little book is lovingly dedicated to my mother and to my son, who were innocently trapped in the occult through their ignorance of the Word of God, and to my niece, Eleanor, from Massachusetts, whom I led to Christian Science, and to my niece, Liselotte

ᐟ Contents

FOREWORD 9

ACKNOWLEDGMENTS 11

FRIED CHICKEN, ANYONE? 15

MANY PATHS TO GOD 17

THE GOOD IS ENEMY OF THE BEST 37
  Summation by Dolores Hayford

EPILOGUE 41

ENDORSEMENTS 43

✐ Foreword

I first met Alice Braemer three years before she wrote her book. It was during registration time at a Women's Aglow Retreat at Springs of Living Water, Richardson Springs, California. More than two hundred laughing, chattering women were to file past the desk, and yet I have a vivid memory of Alice. She was introduced to me as a recent convert out of a metaphysical background. I was struck by a little-girl quality of eagerness and wide-eyed wonder that was almost in contradiction to her air of sophistication and her impeccable grooming.

Later, we received a steady stream of gift subscriptions from her for our periodical, *Testimony* magazine, with the explanation that many of the recipients were in cults or in the occult, but were searchers for Truth, just as she had been. She hoped to point them in the direction of Jesus Christ, who is the only door into that for which they were searching.

Then a few months ago we met again and I was impressed with the undiminished fervor of her desire to witness to those in that gray world where truth and error are so interwoven that neither can be clearly discerned. We agreed to publish Alice's testimony. It was concise and left me feeling there was much more that should be told of her long quest for a personal relationship with God.

Then came the initial manuscript of Alice Braemer's book. As I read it a wave of compassion swept over me for Alice as the bewildered little girl coping with difficult situations, urged on by a growing personal ambition to achieve success in the field of creative arts, yet always looking for answers that would soothe her restless spirit.

As I followed Alice through her marriage and the birth of her only child, I saw her problems becoming almost insurmountable. I grew impatient at the lapses of time, sometimes years, that dragged on between the flashes of light that urged her on in her search for God.

I found myself wishing I could have known Alice in those moments that bordered on despair, but would I have been sensitive enough to have reached past the sophisticated exterior to touch those tender areas so in need of ministry? Perhaps not. But I do know that since reading her first book—for I feel there must eventually be a sequel—I have a desire to communicate with those, like Alice, who are seeking for God in that misty area of cults and the occult. Many speak glibly of God but ignore His Son, who knocks at their heart's door, pleading, "If any man will hear my voice and open the door, I will come in and sup with him, and he with me." Rev. 3:20. May the reading of this book cause many to recognize that persistent knocking and gain the courage to throw open the door and welcome in the Son of God, the Saviour of Mankind!

—RUTH D. NICKEL

✐ Acknowledgments

I praise the Lord that He reveals to us some wonderful individuals to help us along the way:

Dr. Michael Esses, who couldn't possibly know how much his book, *The Phenomenon of Obedience,* meant to me as our family set out for California in 1974, having no idea where we were going to settle down so late in our lives; Dolores Hayford, a great Bible teacher and a wonderful help in editing much of my testimony for AGLOW fellowships, the prisons, and the churches; Tommie and Ruth Nickel, publishers of *Testimony* magazine, the little book that started the wheels turning for this publication; Iverna Tompkins, a tower of strength for me in the Lord and a faithful prayer partner; Pastor Kitely of Shiloh Temple who provided a spiritual haven for our son in their Coffee House each Friday evening; Harold Bredesen, who will be my forever friend in the Lord; Charles Colson for his encouragement; the Reverend Howard Rusthol, radio evangelist, another faithful prayer partner; Margaret Martinez, who gave me my first opportunity to speak for the Women's AGLOW Fellowship in Oakland; and many, many others who gave their moral support and comfort in the dark days.

I WANT TO SHARE THE ACTIVITIES THAT HAVE BLESSED ME:

Christ Church
(Rev. MacArthur Jollay, Pastor)
Massachusetts Ave.
Washington, D. C.

Women's AGLOW Fellowship International
(for the fellowship nearest you, write:)
P. O. Box I
Lynnwood, Wa. 98036

Neighborhood Church
John Drive at Castro Valley Blvd.
Castro Valley, Ca. 94546
(Dr. Jacob M. Bellig, Pastor)

Springs of Living Water
Richardson Springs
California 95973

Shiloh Temple
(Rev. V. Kitely, Pastor)
3521 38th Avenue
Oakland, Ca.

Holy Redeemer Center
8555 Golf Links Road
Oakland, Ca. 94605
(Father Richard Shiblin)

Bible Study Fellowship, Int'l.
5550 Redwood Rd.
Oakland, Ca. 94602
(write for the fellowship nearest you)

From Cultism to Charisma

Fried Chicken
Anyone?

*And I, if I be lifted up from earth, will
draw all men unto me (John 12:32).*

Have you heard the latest? Well, listen to this! It's not
really gossip. It's a fact! There are two victorious, redeemed
people for the Lord! *Right out of the office of Jeane Dixon!*
And the two victorious, redeemed people for the Lord are
Colonel Sanders and I! *Praise the Lord!*

I'm sure "y'all" know who Colonel Sanders is—the fried
chicken man? His picture has been printed in all the news-
papers with Pat Robertson of the "700 Club" television
program.

Back in 1966, at the time I began working with Jeane
Dixon, Colonel Sanders was Chairman of the Board for
Jeane Dixon's Children to Children Foundation. At that
time there was a TV spot being shown almost every half
hour for several months on Channel 7 in Washington, D. C.;
it showed Colonel Sanders and Jeane Dixon acting out a little
skit, explaining to the public how they could throw their
pennies into the fountains of each fried chicken store.

15

Colonel Sanders did not remain very long with Jeane Dixon. I'm sharing this to let you know that the Lord was working in Colonel Sanders's life a little sooner than He worked out the crisis in my life. Colonel Sanders has already published his book, his Christian Testimony, called *Finger Lickin' Good* and he was on the "700 Club" two years before I was. So, I say again, *Praise the Lord* for saving Colonel Sanders and me! *Hallelujah!*

✒ Many Paths to God

Just think! The White House is only a few blocks away from Jeane Dixon's office. It really blows my mind when I realize the Lord was working on Charles Colson, the Watergate, and me all at the same time! Truly, He is no respecter of persons!

Isn't it exciting when we consider the uniqueness of God? We hear testimony after testimony and there are no two alike, so we really cannot compare them. However, some testimonies are more dramatic than others. Well, my testimony is *both* dramatic and traumatic.

I am reminded day after day of what St. Paul said in Phil. 3:13-14, "Brethren, I count not myself to have apprehended: but this one thing I do, forgetting those things which are behind, and reaching forth unto those things which are before, I press toward the mark for the prize of the high calling of God in Christ Jesus." Praise God!

*   *   *

Some individuals consider their testimonies to be just average and not worth sharing, but I truly believe everyone's testimony is important to the Lord, because, when you place them all together, as you would in a jig-saw puzzle, they form a beautiful tapestry for the glory of God.

Each time I give my testimony several individuals express real amazement that someone like me, who had been a close associate of Jeane Dixon for seven years—traveling with her, living with her much of the time, and knowing about all the things that take place behind the scenes of someone who was so much in the public eye and having a part in the excitement of such a life as Jeane Dixon's—could be saved! They say, "How did you come to get interested in genuine, old-fashioned Spirit-filled, Christian living? How did God catch your attention long enough to come into your life?" *Well, only Jesus could do that!* But, when it is put to me in the form of a direct question like that, I am reminded of the *shock* of the incident that actually brought me to my knees—to Jesus. It comes back to me with terrific impact! This, of course, was the terrible condition of our son Carlton. (Please continue to pray for him, that God may use him for His glory!)

You see, I realize there had to be a cause for Carlton's condition, so I want to get back to the *cause*, and that leads me back into the formative years of my own childhood. I know now that the formative years of my childhood had a far greater part in my finally coming to Jesus than many of the things which I *thought* were pressing me to a spiritual awakening.

I truly believe it is important to share my testimony with you because of the tremendous burden I have to warn people about the occult, since our whole nation—yes, our whole nation—is so involved with things of this nature. I'm speaking about the Ouija board, astrology, fortune telling, reading palms, analyzing handwriting, E.S.P., numerology, flying saucers and magic, yes magic, *all* those things that look so innocent and harmless. I want to warn as many people as I can get to listen to me—*to leave those things strictly alone!* They can bring nothing but trouble, sorrow, and grief. Then mental hospitals are filled with such misled people!

For those seeking the truth about occultism, I highly recommend books by Dr. Kurt Koch, reported to be a close friend of Billy Graham. His book *Christian Counselling and Occultism* is an investigation covering medicine, psychiatry, psychology, depth psychology, religious psychology, parapsychology and theology. For books on the cults, I strongly recommend the books of Dr. Walter Martin of the Melodyland School of Theology in Anaheim, California. Also, please read Richard DeHaan's book, *Satan, Satanism and Witchcraft.*

*   *   *

The mental hospitals are so overcrowded, the patients can no longer remain there. They are given medication and sent out into the world again.

I know for an absolute fact that many psychics have been placed on the Board of Directors at State Mental Hospitals so it is important to know about the occult.

I know also, that there are lecture bureaus all across the United States for the psychics, under the name of Spiritual Frontiers Fellowship, which was started by the late Arthur Ford.

Surely, some of the Christians could assume the burden for Christian speaker's bureaus across the country, so that new Christians may share their testimonies more freely.

My mother and father are still alive today and praise God they are born-again believers in Jesus Christ! They have been married seventy years and are now in their nineties.

My mother was always a religious woman and when I say *religious,* I mean she was a strict disciple of the rituals of the Roman Catholic Church. But, you see, there was no *real* knowledge of God and His *love* in her life. She truly believed that the Roman Catholic Church was the only, only way of salvation and as long as you belonged to *that* church and fulfilled the demands it required of you, well, *that* was all *God* required.

Very early in our childhood my mother would get us up daily at 6:00 A.M. to go with her to early mass. Well, I certainly didn't get anything out of the services. How could I possibly relate to the services when they were all read in Latin? However, I am grateful for the self-discipline that I learned as a result of some of these practices of my early childhood. If nothing else, it certainly instilled an awareness of God deep within me and I do recall, as I sat there in the church, my eyes were always focused on the gigantic replica of the crucifixion, which was placed directly back of the altar.

No one ever told me that I would inherit eternal life because of Jesus' suffering. I know I felt a deep indignation that He was brutally treated when He deserved nothing but good, and I know I could feel the love of Jesus gently entering my heart, and I needed to express this love by painting pictures of Jesus.

I have mentioned before that my mother insisted on all these rituals of the church being observed—but at *home* our life was beyond belief! My mother and father argued constantly—*constantly!* The turmoil and chaos in our home were so distressing to me that I would go up into the attic just to get away from the noise and hateful atmosphere of our home.

My mother was also interested in metaphysical literature, but she seldom had time to read it. However, she *did* take the time occasionally to read the cards and tell fortunes and read the tea leaves. This is not in the least uncommon among a large percentage of churchgoing people.

You see, we didn't have the Word of God in our home and we didn't have the Word of God in our church, so my mother had no way of knowing about Leviticus 19:31 where it tells us, "Regard not them that have familiar spirits, neither seek after wizards, to be defiled by them: I am the Lord your God."

People have no real understanding of the Scriptures—it is a trick of Satan to prevent people from getting any real spiritual benefit from their churchgoing activities.

There is a way to a happy marriage and Colossians 3:18-19 points out the way when it states, "Wives, submit yourselves unto your own husbands, as it is fit in the Lord. Husbands, love your wives, and be not bitter against them."

Whatever rules my parents were taught to observe they faithfully practiced. If my mother had known that her pursuit of fortune-telling was an abomination to God, I am sure she would have been the first to confess her sin but she did not even *know* it was a sin! As a matter of fact she was told it was a *gift!*

Now that I know there are such things as evil spirits, I am convinced that my mother was being *used* by such forces. She told us that she was born with a veil over her face which enabled her to see people and events that others could not see. Her violent temper, so often vented against family members, reveals clearly the oppression of demonic nature.

*   *   *

In trying to reach back into the very beginning of the Lord Jesus' efforts toward me, I recall a picture I was working on up in our attic at the time I was about seven or eight years of age—and I know *now* it was really Jesus drawing me to Himself. By grace He first loved me. My heart would have rejoiced if I had known about John 15:16, "Ye have not chosen me, but I have chosen you, and ordained you, that ye should go and bring forth fruit, and that your fruit should remain: that whatsoever ye shall ask of the Father in my name, he may give it you."

The happiness I experienced while I was up in the attic is indescribable. The picture I was painting was a sad one and was called "The Sacred Heart of Jesus." The eyes were looking upward towards heaven and the crown of thorns was causing the blood to drip down on His face and His heart was exposed and bleeding. I can remember crying very often.

One day, while I was working on the face of Jesus, the Lord appeared to me right through that sad painting! He was smiling and seemed to be saying to me, "Now I am a risen Christ Alice and I *love* you." This wonderful vision of my Lord had a profound effect on my later life especially in times of trials, and temptations, and crises, when I really needed such comfort.

Isn't it wonderful how patiently and faithfully the Lord will work, bringing us around to a *real knowledge* of Himself! In spite of the fact that the Lord had proven himself a friend to me, I was still totally blind to the real spiritual truths he would want me to know. I would no sooner come down from my quiet times of drawing and the sense of peace that I always felt up there in the attic, when I would pick up some book on metaphysics that was lying around our house—and anyone who has read metaphysics and Eastern religions knows that the devil is declared to be a myth. They say, "There is no devil!" Now, if I had been taught the Word of God I would have known all about I Peter 5:8, "Be sober, be vigilant; because your adversary the devil, as a roaring lion, walketh about, seeking whom he may devour."

*   *   *

I remember the time when the neighbors asked my mother why I spent so much time alone in the attic while other children were out playing and I can hear her so clearly as she replied, "Alice is a very old soul. She has come back to the earth to remind the people of the love of Jesus." That was the first time I had ever heard of reincarnation. I truly thought *everyone* believed that way; I just took it in my stride and promptly forgot about it. Hebrews 9:27, if I had known the Word of God, could have prevented me from being deceived, for it is written, "And it is appointed unto men once to die, but after this the judgment." Oh, the tragedy of not knowing the Word of God!

The Lord knows that children are most certainly going to be largely the result of the principles on which they were raised. I can really see the truth of that, in thinking over my own life.

As I began to get interested in movies and movie stars, I yearned to have a career of my own. My mother arranged for me to have lessons to develop whatever talents I might have and while I did not get into show biz as such, I did finally make a career for myself in modeling expensive clothing.

The fantasies I had imagined as I posed before my mirror at home as a little girl were much, much closer to reality then. In the fine shops where I was employed, I was modeling for such people as Eleanor Roosevelt, Barbara Hutton, the Vanderbilts, the Mayor of New York City and his wife, and all the movie stars and VIPs of that day. It was so exciting, I loved every minute of it! I was so young I didn't know any better and in looking back now, I can only be thankful that I didn't get into show business as such. I am convinced that at least my morals were less compromised, going this route, even though my dreams were in the direction of Hollywood. *I praise God that he kept his mighty hand upon me.*

*   *   *

Among other things that had been available for my reading while yet at home was *Unity* literature. There are very few people who have not read *Unity* literature of one sort or another or, possibly, Eastern religions or TM and perhaps the hardest thing about testimonies of this nature is realizing that it is beautiful material and it has a soothing effect on the one reading it. Perhaps the reader, right now, is offended that I classify it as *false* teaching. Please, if this is the case, do hear me with an open mind—for you are traveling my very path! And it does have a great deal of truth in it! Unity groups even refer to themselves as the Unity School of Truth or the Unity School of Christianity. But there is no *real* truth outside of a right knowledge of Jesus, who declared Himself to be not only the Truth but the Way and most importantly, the Life.

Unity literature appealed to me because of the loveliness of its message. But in my pursuit of its harmonious teachings, I was being led farther and farther away from *real* truth, for with my lack of scriptural understanding, I was quite ready to accept the fact that there is NO DEVIL. There is no real evil—evil is just the absence of Light—they taught me and I did not know that God's Word says men love darkness because their deeds are evil and they do not want to be exposed to the light. We know the light is Jesus! "I am the Light of the World, He declared, and he that cometh to Me shall receive the Light of Life!"

You see, the devil is far too smart to ever attack us in areas that are strong! Here I was, since childhood definitely interested in spiritual things and the devil saw to it that my searching would appear to be satisfied. My reaching out for loveliness was perfectly all right with Satan, just so long as I did not find the "fairest of ten thousand"—and who is the "fairest of ten thousand?" The Lord Jesus!

*   *   *

There is much that could be said and actually things that you should know if indeed in your home, there is any recognition or acceptance of the occult, or of religious material or objects, that are not scripturally sound. I'm thinking, at the moment, about those numerous statues of Buddha with the fat, round belly that are supposed to be so "neat," so "chic" with interior decorators. If you do have such things you are moving in the realm of the satanic, regardless of how pleasant or fascinating it may seem to you at the moment.

God has spoken to us this warning in I Peter 5:8, "Be sober, be vigilant, because your adversary the devil, as a roaring lion, walketh about, seeking whom he may devour." Now God has not spoken these works just to make an exciting illustration. It is an *invariable,* and I mean an invariable, truth that if you embrace the serpent, eventually he will strike! His one purpose is to prevent you from receiving eternal life. *HIS ONE PURPOSE IS TO PREVENT YOU FROM RECEIVING ETERNAL LIFE.* If you swallow Satan's "pretty pills" that route suits him just fine! But believe me, the path does not *stay* rosy for once you are immersed in the satanic, regardless of how harmless it appears on the surface, you can count on the fact that it will go with you wherever you go!

When I left my family home to make my own way in the world, little did I dream how true that would be. Goodness knows this satanic force tried to keep me in its grip, as I was plagued with migraine headaches for many years. Also, my sister—my beautiful, beautiful sister—committed suicide and we all agree, I'm sure, that the compulsion to take one's own life is most certainly not of God but of the enemy. The very confusion that caused me to escape, by retreating to the attic, perhaps settled more deeply upon her. Always, there is the feeling of sadness upon such a death and the terrible guilt of those remaining, who wonder if they were part of the cause.

*   *   *

I do want to tell you more about Eleanor Roosevelt now. She had the priceless quality of making people feel important and worthwhile. She was always eager to help people and she even reached out to try to help nations. Now, are you ready for this? She put her stamp of approval on an activity—a world-wide activity that seems to be so worthy, so noble! She called it a "beautiful concept" and in my ignorance of God's Word, I agreed with her and I stupidly supported this activity with my money and with all the zeal of an evangelist. The activity is called The Temple of Understanding and it is comprised of *all* the leaders of *all* the religions of *all* the world. The land for this activity, which was purchased through Jeane Dixon's office, was dedicated on the sixth day of the sixth month in the year of 1966—and guess what? They have the approval and blessings of the United Nations! So the stage is all set for the coming of the anti-Christ. Why am I telling you all this, because I must let you know it's later, much later, than we think!

*   *   *

While living alone in New York City, I was led to reside at the Allerton House. It was really an international hotel, where people from all over the world could meet and some-times those meetings led to marriage.

I asked the Lord to reveal to me if my "Prince Charming" was among the residents. I had only been living there *one* week and lo and behold! there he was, right on schedule, according to the Lord's timetable. He introduced himself as Carlo Braemer and told me he had been living with his aunt, the Baroness Alma Dahlrup—you can imagine how im-pressed I was! After all, I was just a small-town girl and my values at that time were probably centered on self-preserva-tion and the glamour of the world. BUT PRAISE GOD, *JESUS IS EVERYTHING* TO ME NOW!

During the course of our conversation Carlo informed me that his aunt, the Baroness was the president and founder of the American Scandinavian Society, which is nation-wide in scope. She also had the statue of Hans Christian Andersen erected in Central Park.

I was just thrilled to hear all this and within two weeks Carlo asked me to marry him. Six months later we were united in matrimony in the rectory of a Roman Catholic church in New York City.

*   *   *

We spent our honeymoon in Europe and visited Carlo's family in Denmark. It was so wonderful to learn that he came from such a fine family. I was surprised to hear that Carlo's younger sister Lis was born exactly ten years later than Carlo, but the amazing thing about it is (and I have never heard anything quite like this before), they both have *the same birthday!* Only the Lord could cause such a strange coincidence!

Lis had just married a man named George Albeck, whose father had founded the University of Aarhus. George had an excellent job with the Danish Government. It was a position that brought him into close contact with King Frederick of Denmark. Lis and George were royally entertained at the palace by the king and queen over a long period of time, until the death of the king about ten years ago. Their daughter Lisalotte was a classmate of the royal Princess Bernadette.

There were many dinner parties in our honor during our honeymoon, and many castles to visit, and so much to see! Our honeymoon was over all too soon!

During the next six years of our marriage I continued to be a fashion model but, oh, how I longed for a child!

I had become interested in Christian Science and was teaching Bible stories to little children in the neighborhood. The story of Hannah in the Bible was constantly before me— how she longed for a child and how she dedicated him to the Lord before he was born. So I decided to do the very same thing. Finally, it happened! I was going to have a baby!

I remember how serene I felt during the pregnancy except for the last few months before the birth, when the child in my womb was wildly active, jumping around with fierce motion. I blissfully said to Carlo, "This child will be about the Father's business." (I still haven't given up on that statement, regardless of all that has happened in the past.)

Christian Science appeared to be a discipline necessary for my mental and physical health—no pills, no medication, no smoking, no drinking—but alas, there was also no Lucifer, no devil, only "mortal mind" and "error." I just kept on reading the literature and the lessons, all day practically, to saturate my consciousness with positive statements of truth. *This is a far cry from feasting on the word of God.*

Our son Carlton was quite a shock to us. He kept us so busy. He had us jumping around serving him. I suppose today it is called "hyperactive." He had a strong, willful nature and was stubborn beyond all imagination. Carlo and I wondered why he never did any creeping as a baby. He just got up and walked, with his hands sliding along the wall to support himself. He never fell asleep like other children—not until he was quite ready—and comfortably settled in his own crib. He was a torment to us in many ways and it was so bad—the conflict between us—that I began to get crying spells. I cried so much that I finally asked my husband to send me away to a sanitarium.

Carlo could see the danger signals ahead and he quickly enrolled Carlton in a nursery school right around the corner from our apartment building. It was then agreed between us that I would go back to the business world.

*   *   *

Carlton was just a little boy when I had my second vision of Jesus. It took place at the exact time Oral Roberts emerged

on the scene with his tent crusades and his television programs, preaching the gospel and healing the sick. I have been
supporting Oral Roberts's ministry since 1947.

We had an apartment in Kew Gardens, New York. I
always slept alone in the foyer because I was a light sleeper,
while Carlo and Carlton slept in the one bedroom.

One morning early, about six o'clock, while I was on the
verge of waking up, I became aware of the fact that the birds
outside my window were all singing merrily. Suddenly I
heard the sound of a "click" and I looked up. There, right
before my eyes, stood Jesus in all His radiance and glory and
splendor and majesty, *smiling at me!*

The vision lasted about twenty seconds, only to me it was
far more than a vision, because there was dimension and color
involved in this visitation. I was gloriously surprised and
happy!

I jumped up and went into the bathroom and closed the
door, in order to contemplate the joy that flooded my soul!
Then, I asked the Father why He had shown me the Son. The
impression I received was just three words, *"Feed my Sheep."*
Well, I thought that meant that I was to go into the Sunday
School and teach the children the Bible stories, so I took the
necessary steps to bring it about.

*   *   *

I had many fine jobs over the years while Carlton was
growing up, and one of them was that of saleslady at the
Elizabeth Arden Salon in Washington, D. C. Right at this
point I would like to explain why I was motivated to remain
with Jeane Dixon for seven years. One day while I was working at Elizabeth Arden's a friend of Jeane Dixon's came in
to make a purchase. Somehow the conversation led to my
interest in children and, of course, the Bible stories. Jeane

Dixon has a cat named "Mike the MagiCat." Now her ambition was to see the cat brought forth in books: children's
books, comic strips, TV programs, balloons, chewing gum,
wrist watches, toys, etc. She wanted "Mike the MagiCat" to
be just like Mickey Mouse and bring in large sums of money.
Jeane Dixon was supposed to build a hospital for children
for $125,000,000. Well, I was inspired, really inspired (may-
be *obsessed* is a better word) to combine the children's Bible
stories, which I had used in the Sunday Schools for twenty-
five years, with "Mike the MagiCat." Mike was to be the
teacher and the children were to be his students.

In retrospect, I can see that the Lord would not be too
pleased with a *cat* teaching Bible stories but at that time, I
thought the puppet-type approach would appeal to children.
So, *that* was my motive (my big hang-up) for working so
patiently with Jeane Dixon—*I really thought she would
eventually publish the Bible stories.*

When I explained my plan to Jeane Dixon's friend that
day at Elizabeth Arden's Salon she was enchanted with the
idea and insisted that I prepare myself to have lunch with
Jeane Dixon the following day. The subject of our conversation was naturally to be about the Bible stories. Well, it never
happened that way at all! When Jeane Dixon and I finally
met she didn't want to discuss *Bible stories* but she *was* interested to learn that I was preparing to take my real estate
examination. You see, Jeane Dixon is in the real estate business with her husband. She is a broker and she therefore
suggested that I work in her office after I obtained my license.
I did not remain in her real estate office very long and it was
about a year later that she unexpectedly asked me to accom-
pany her on a speaking-engagement flight across the country.
We were very harmonious in our combined efforts for her
success. As I mentioned before, Jeane Dixon was supposed to
build a hospital for children and she realized I was eager to

assist her in every way so she offered me the job to travel exclusively with her on a full time basis.

The work was so exciting! We met wonderful people everywhere. My job was to set up the press conferences in each city, to take pictures of all the special dignitaries, tape her lectures and write up a complete report concerning everything that happened—all the persons, places and things pertaining to each trip.

Jeane Dixon, over a period of seven years, was in the company of the president of the United States, the president of Mexico, and the president of Austria.

She spent time with many of the governors and mayors throughout the country, as well as Members of Congress. Jeane Dixon spoke in Hawaii and Canada, Alaska and Vienna, Austria. She appeared at the Hollywood Bowl and was on all the talk shows across the country. Many of the church denominations invited her to speak, among them was the Roman Catholic Church and the Unity Metaphysical Church. We traveled as often as three times a week.

I was always placed at the head table. Jeane Dixon tried many times to prevent this but she could not succeed. The people who invited her, *insisted* that I sit at the head table. She referred to me as her *opposing viewpoint*. *There never was a moment that I didn't have a sense of destiny because of my two visions of Jesus.* I earnestly tried for seven years to interest Jeane Dixon in publishing the Bible stories but it just didn't work out! It was a lost cause! *GOD HAD OTHER PLANS!*

*   *   *

At the end of the seven years, although I didn't realize what was happening at the time, a crisis was about to take place in our home and in our lives that would cause a tre-

mendous shakeup—a complete change in location and life-
style!

For two years prior to the crisis, and right up to the
shock of Carlton's condition, I had been listening *constantly*
to Oral Roberts's tapes on the subject of "The Holy Spirit in
the Now." Just at this point in time Oral Roberts and the
teachers of Oral Roberts University were discussing demon
possession on the tapes. Just think! No one had ever mentioned demons to us before and no one had ever warned me
about Jeane Dixon, or the occult and no one had ever wit-
nessed to us about the Lord Jesus.

Meanwhile, over the years, Carlton had been under the
care of psychiatrists and as a child he had visited his grand-
mother every summer. He was such a restless and demanding
youngster that my mother thought she could amuse him by
showing him how to read fortunes and tea leaves. Also, my
brother Stephen had been studying hypnotism and was always
eager to practice on our son.

We didn't think too much about it when Carlton went
out and bought his own pack of cards and purchased his own
tea and tea cup. But one thing led to another and before
we knew it, Carlton was going to the Library of Congress to
find out about witchcraft. By that time he had also been
committed to the mental hospital from which he was later
released.

Carlton was a terrible problem to us. We never could un-
derstand what went wrong and no one can imagine the con-
stant fear and terror I went through year after year, because
we never knew when he would become violent. Since we
were students of Christian Science, it just never occurred
to us that Carlton's problem was demonic, until that fateful
day when I heard him giggling in his room and invoking the
name of Lucifer! That did it! Instantly, *instantly,* a veil was

torn from my eyes. I could see clearly, for the first time, that Satan was alive and well on the planet Earth.

Nothing will ever be the same for us. It was the *point of no return* the *crisis*—the *crossroads*—the *turning point in our lives! In my despair I cried out to God, and in His mercy, He rescued us.*

* * *

Praise the Lord! A few days later, I tuned into the "700 Club" TV program from Washington, D. C. and Pat Robertson invited everyone to kneel down in their homes and give their hearts to Jesus. I have been doing so ever since. Every time he says "kneel down" I drop down on my knees, because I have come into the Body of Christ so late in my life that I want to be sure I haven't missed the boat!

It wasn't long before I was enjoying other programs on the Christian Broadcasting Network, such programs as "Charisma," "The Happy Hunters," "Kathryn Kuhlman," "Oral Roberts" and other programs.

* * *

My husband and I never cease to be amazed that the very son who brought us so much trouble and heartache over the years is the one the Lord used to awaken us and bring us to Jesus. What can we say but Praise God!

I received the baptism in the Holy Spirit and my new prayer language a few years ago after attending a Roman Catholic Charismatic meeting at St. Michael's Church in Annandale, Virginia.

During the last few years, we have all been attending Full Gospel Churches and Prayer Groups, Bible College,

Aglow Fellowship, Bible Study Fellowship, and the Full Gospel Business Men's Breakfast. Our son Carlton enjoys the young people at Shiloh Temple and he is sure to be at their coffee house each Friday evening, in Oakland. We have attended the Neighborhood Church in Castro Valley during the past year.

*   *   *

In the summer of 1975, our family drove to Anaheim to attend the Full Gospel Business Men's International Convention. Carlton was with us and he seemed to be in a state of catatonia. His mouth was open and his hands slightly rigid. He was a sorry sight to behold and there was no way of hiding his six-feet-three-inch presence. I remember thinking, "If Carlo and I have any false pride, this condition of Carlton's will certainly yank it out of us."

When we arrived in Anaheim on the morning of June 30th, we decided to inspect the Convention Center. The only people around at that time were Demos Shakarian, the president and his vice-president, Thomas Ashcraft. We had an opportunity to have a brief conversation with them. That was the beginning of how the Lord led us to be right up close to the various speakers and leaders.

I met a lady named Ruth Crandall who offered me her luncheon ticket. (I had first known Ruth several years before when Jeane Dixon spoke in Pittsburgh, Pennsylvania, and Ruth had come to see her.) Well, Ruth had to leave town unexpectedly and she graciously and generously gave me her reserved seat luncheon ticket.

What a surprise to find myself right up close to the head table and very close to both Evelyn Roberts and Maude Aimee Humbard. If I had known in advance what was about to happen, I would have raced out of the room!

When it was Maude Aimee's time to speak—she began to tell her audience how weary she was from constantly packing her traveling bags and going off to faraway places with her husband, Rex Humbard. Just at that point I began to feel uneasy. I was thinking how weary I was sometimes as I was packing my luggage, returning with Jeane Dixon after a faraway speaking engagement with only two or three hours sleep. All at once, as Maude Aimee Humbard was singing "He's the Saviour of My Soul," I felt the conviction of the Holy Spirit come upon me. He seemed to be saying, "You have packed your bags many, many times in the past—are you ready to pack your bags for the Lord?" And just then, without any warning, a great sorrow gripped me and over-whelmed me. The tears began to splash out of my eyes and all I wanted to do was just get down on the floor and cry my eyes out. I thought to myself, "I've always been so much in command of my emotions and now I seem so powerless!"

I quickly grasped the situation and knew I didn't want to create a disturbance at this lovely luncheon so I pleaded, "Lord if you will just stop this flood of tears, I'll promise to be ready, at a moment's notice, to pack my traveling bags for you all the days of my life." The memory of this experience will be with me always because of the wonderful cleansing process that had taken place within me.

*   *   *

Following the convention, another happy event took place. Dolores and Jack Hayford opened up their home to us and to a group of dedicated Christians for prayer and study over a period of thirteen weeks. I am so very grateful for this because my husband is a new person in Christ. He treats me with brand new love and respect. Carlo acts as though we are on our honeymoon after all these years! It's really wonderful the way we pray together every evening, and tell each other that we still care about each other, in the love of the Lord.

A real Christian ministry has unfolded in my life now. I am telling my story, my testimony, on both television and radio and at the Women's AGLOW Fellowships and in the churches. Another ministry that is so fulfilling to me is the prison work with Teen Challenge.

: I will soon be returning to the Federal Center where Patty Hearst is serving her term . . . and sometimes I think of the multitudes of people that Patty could lead to JESUS, and very softly in my heart I hear His words (John 12:32), "And I, if I be lifted up from the earth, will draw all men unto me."

The Good Is the Enemy of the Best

SUMMATION BY DOLORES HAYFORD

Having heard Alice give her testimony, and having had many personal conversations with her regarding different aspects of her life, I can only say, God is faithful to the promise of His Word!

No matter how far from His royal highway her pursuits may have taken her, God is not as man who looks upon the outward appearance. He is the Creator who deals according to the intents of the heart.

As faulty as her understanding was, with regard to God's plan for all of us to come to Him through the blood of His Son, Jesus, He did not forsake the little girl who had no one to interpret the first dealings of the Holy Spirit when she "felt sorry for the sufferings of Jesus" and when she knew no other way to express worship than to make paintings of the Lord.

How important it is for parents to be able to introduce their children to the Living Jesus who loves little children, and longs to become their Lord in those years when the

heart is tender and open. "Suffer the little children to come
unto me, and forbid them not: for of such is the kingdom of
God" (Mark 10:14). But there was no one to do that for
Alice; well-meaning as her mother was, she had nothing but
ritual. She, herself, was feeding on the false doctrines of
metaphysics and the occult in an effort to satisfy that hunger
that is built into the heart of humanity, "but how shall they
hear without a preacher" (Romans 10:14).

Having read intensively in metaphysical literature that
there is *no evil,* and that knowing the Truth will set you free,
Alice was a ripe candidate for Christian Science, with their
emphasis on healing. Migraine headaches were almost
her physical and emotional undoing after she had gone to
New York to pursue a modeling career. And in Christian
Science she was taught how to discipline the *mind* and rule
over one's own symptoms and emotional hurts. Here again,
however, was "the letter that killeth," rather than the spirit
which gives life. In the intensive program of study of the
Scriptures, as interpreted by the founder of the organization
one is only instructed to "affirm" these Scriptures of positive
promise. No introduction to Jesus who proclaims of Himself,
"I am the Way and the Truth and the Life." We Christians
are so prone to give up on the multiplied thousands of people
who are trapped in these high sounding, beautiful-speaking
religions! Praise the Lord, He is ever searching the hearts!

First, no parents to teach her, second, no church to teach
her—God used the very thing that attracted her to Christian
Science to provoke her attention to His message—Oral
Roberts Healing Ministry of prayer for the sick, and the fact
that he taught God is a *good* God appealed to her, but when
he said the devil is a *bad* devil, it went right over Alice's head
because she had been trained to believe otherwise. Her thinking *was* disciplined, *was* dedicated but was *sterile!*

It was not until 1973 when Oral Roberts went into detail

about demon possession on his tapes that she caught the impact of the devil being a *bad* devil.

Simultaneously and strangely enough, Carlton, the child she had so longed for, but whose own emotional problems had been more than she could handle, would be the one to ultimately shock her into the reality of Spiritual Truth. There was no doubt that something far from *good* was driving this child to distraction, almost from infancy. Alice, who did not even know how to pray herself—but who had been taught to believe that you disciplined yourself to *know* truth and thus appropriate it—heard this son calling on the prince of the powers of darkness and suddenly found the things Oral Roberts had been saying made far more sense than the platitudes of Christian Science and other metaphysical teaching.

And thus it is that after her life was more than half spent, the real *TRUTH*—Jesus—was finally uncovered through the faithfulness of a compassionate God who knows the end from the beginning.

You, too, could be finishing this book just now very much in the same condition as Alice was for most of the years of her life. You may have been devoted to the beautiful writings about the God who is Love and who could not *possibly* allow anything but *good* to come to us. It is Alice's challenge that you stop right now and ask yourself the question that you have avoided for so long: If that is true what in the world is happening all around you?

Jesus spoke frequently about the adversary who would steal your very soul. Paul in his writings, gives detailed instruction to believers, so that they need never again suffer the afflictions of Satan and his demons.

You may be trusting in your astrological projections, not realizing that evil forces are so bound up on this sort of thing that it is small wonder they frequently seem to be so. After all, Satan is not so great a fool that he thinks any man will swallow a *total* lie. He mixes much Scripture into his various traps, because it is invariably the seekers after Truth who get very deeply involved in any of the cults and occult teachings. The pitiful situation is *this*—man, in his fallen nature, is *not* looking for a God to serve, he is looking for a God to serve *him*. All these false doctrines offer that kind of promise. *You* can be the master of your fate! *YOU* have the power of God within you. *YOU, YOU, YOU. ME, ME, ME. I, I, I.*

Jesus is the door. Jesus is the Light of life. Jesus is the Bread of Life. Jesus is the Way—mind you, *not* the Way-show-er, but the Way. You must be *in* Him. He must be in *you*. No man will ever arrive at the Father's house unless the Son has ransomed him and Jesus, Himself, leads the errant back home.

Don't be deceived with something that seems better than the last thing you tried:

God will settle for *nothing* but the *best*. That *best* is His own provision, Eternal Life through Jesus, His son.

Alice has found it—
Her parents now have found it—
Her son has found it, and her husband—
                                        Have you?

✐ Epilogue

As you were reading my testimony, did you wonder how many people were really moving out of the cults and how many were being delivered from the damage of the occult?

If this has happened to you, would you share what is taking place in your life, as it will be used in a subsequent book to bless others.

For Example:

If my friend Lois Shinn, who attends Women's AGLOW Fellowship with me, had known Jesus, and all that she knows today about the occult, her darling sister would still be alive. Lois was formerly a student of Unity and Religious Science.

Her sister became involved in a meditation group which delved into the mysteries of the Orient by concentration, chants and incantations. She pursued these studies avidly, searching for answers to give meaning and purpose to her life.

Being of a highly sensitive nature, and after months of practicing these demonic rituals, she gradually became deeply depressed and finally lapsed into a state of catatonia from which she never recovered. Her sister's death brought great sorrow to Lois but we praise the Lord that Lois found Jesus as a result of shopping at Capwell's in Oakland. Lois was looking for a book by Edgar Cayce but the Holy Spirit gently urged her to select instead a book entitled *I Believe in Miracles* by Kathryn Kuhlman. Hallelujah!

At the present time, my husband and I are living in a condominium where we share the swimming pool and recreation area with several other residents.

One day, while I was feeding the ducks in the lagoon, a little girl named Bernadette Branscum joined me and we talked about Jesus.

A few months later I showed her my testimony published by Thomas and Ruth Nickel. The name of the magazine is entitled *Testimony*. Bernadette was very interested and immediately told me about a slumber party she attended last year when she was only eight years old. It was the twelfth birthday of her friend Christy. I was shocked to learn that all the children took part in the practice of levitation and they actually saw a young child rise up off the floor.

This little Bernadette knew all about seances and the young people who were taking part in such activities. No one had ever told her how dangerous the occult is and that it is an abomination to God. What can we do to alert the parents?

Comments, inquiries and requests for speaking engagements should be directed to:

> *Alice Braemer*
> *Box 1105*
> *Alameda, CA 94501*

✓ Endorsements

Is it really possible to have a longing in your heart for the true and living God and in your search for Him to stumble into the occult finding only the counterfeit while longing for the real? To a person of my background, born and raised in a Christian home by Christian parents, it seems the answer to that question would be a severe "no." Alice Braemer did not have the opportunities that I had and asked this same question; her answer would just as emphatically state, "yes." In these days when God is seeking to break down every prejudice and to bring His people up from a legalistic judgmental position to a compassionate understanding one, Alice Braemer's testimony is a "must" for every reader. Those with no involvement or interest in the occult must surely know that it can no longer be ignored and this testimony will shed light that is so necessary for our understanding. Those who have once dabbled in the occult and find lingering questions will possibly discover their answers in this little book and those who presently are involved with any arm of the occult or deceived into believing soul power is sufficient for eternal life absolutely must take the time to read this honest, open story of how Alice Braemer found the truth and has embraced Him to find completeness and happiness that for so long she sought. I personally recommend this book.

IVERNA M. TOMPKINS

Have you ever tried to share Christ with someone involved in metaphysics or the occult, and realized you were talking to deaf ears? They just weren't open to you, because they felt that you had never experienced what they had experienced, or seen what they had seen.

Having experienced that kind of frustration several times myself, I have found that the best way to reach such people is by giving them the testimony of someone who has experienced what they have experienced and seen what they have seen, and then have their eyes opened.

I am convinced that God has permitted Alice Braemer to have all the experiences that she had in the occult to provide her with credentials she could use in rescuing such victims. I highly recommend her book.

Fraternally in Christ,
(Signed) HARALD BREDESEN
Host, "Charisma"
The Christian Broadcasting Network, Inc.

I have just finished reading the manuscript for Alice Braemer's book. It is very readable, interesting, informative, and greatly needed in this day of religious sophistication.

It would be impossible for me to write as Alice has written. My parents were God-fearing Christians and I have always been exposed to the love and reality of God, and the power of His saving grace through faith and acceptance of His Son, the Lord Jesus Christ.

Alice writes her personal experiences, dating back to her childhood, of being involved and exposed to many "religions" but not knowing the "power of God unto salvation." She understands, and thus writes about, the pitfalls and dangers of the occult. Her testimony is a warning to those who are unaware of Satan's subtle ways of deception.

I thank God that she has been "led of the Lord" to put this personal testimony in print. Without hesitation I heartily endorse and recommend it, and trust it will be read by multitudes . . . to the honor and glory of God

HOWARD RUSTHOI